Lean Management for Beginners

Fundamentals of Lean Management for Small and Medium-Sized Enterprises - with many practical examples

Maximilian Tündermann

Table of Contents

1. Introduction

When the founder of an Indian bank wondered why fewer and fewer customers were applying for credit, he looked at the process that regulated the mortgage application. President Jairam Sridharan found out that such a request went through a total of 30 hands. No wonder no one wanted to wait that long. Axis Bank was looking for solutions and ultimately found them not through technology but through philosophy: Lean Management. This Japanese production method is now also used in management and the service industry. The core is that nothing should be wasted. The word lean means slim, and in most cases companies and enterprises are actually slimmed down.

Size doesn't matter, for small and medium-sized companies it may even be easier to slim down because you're not that big. However, streamlining does not necessarily mean saving costs, dismissing or outsourcing personnel, or closing business areas. The difference between the classic lean approach and the lean approach is that it is process oriented. Leaning is only done where it is necessary to improve the process. It is also possible that only the processes themselves may be changed, without really incurring costs.

If you run a company today, you'll soon find that two or three years after its foundation, some sort of routine becomes apparent. Business is going well—hopefully—customers are satisfied, sales are growing, and so is profit. It is precisely at this stage that many companies begin to expand their organization, build up bureaucratic hurdles and, pampered by success, no longer reflect on themselves. With Lean Management, conversely, this danger is minimized because it involves a constant improvement, with which there is no leaning back.

This book is intended to give you insights into Lean Management and help you understand it. Examples from other companies can help you to think about the introduction of Lean Management yourself or to first analyze how and where it can be used in your company.

2. History of Lean Manufacturing

You can only understand Lean Management if you know where it comes from. The origins lie in lean manufacturing, which was mainly developed by Japanese car manufacturers. The Toyota production system, which is primarily concerned with avoiding and minimizing waste, is still being used worldwide today and has been copied by many competitors. Toyoda Sackichi developed the system back in 1902, but it was constantly improved. His son Kiichiro then formed the just-in-time idea, which was only produced according to demand. This was also necessary because there were hardly any raw materials at that time and some markets were not accessible to the Japanese because of war. The carmakers had no choice but to save resources if they wanted to boost the economy again. It was the engineer Taiichi Ohno who developed a production method based on these considerations, whose main goal was to avoid waste: "The starting concept of the Toyota production system was, as I have emphasized several times, a thorough elimination of waste."[1]

---

[1] Ohno, T. (1988): *Toyota Production System – Beyond Large-Scale Production*, Productivity Press, Cambridge/Massachusetts

The ultimate goal is to increase productivity without compromising quality and delivery times. The **Jidoka** principle is one of the pillars that ensures quality through a process whereby errors are detected and eliminated at an early stage. This includes

- Stop production

- Make manuals

- Error message

The second pillar is **just-in-time production**: it is only done when it is needed, in the quantity that is needed and as required by the customer. On the one hand, this establishes the principle of customer focus but on the other it also avoids waste. Components of this pillar are:

- Produce only for customers, not for stock (Build to Order)

- Pull instead of Push

- Continuous flow of materials and resources

- Suitable and flexibly deployable employees

Avoiding waste was the main concern of car manufacturers, particularly because it directly affected value creation. For this reason, they formulated the most important types of waste:

- Overproduction

- Material stocks

- Transports and routes

- Cumbersome processing

- Cumbersome movements

- Waiting times

- Rework

So Lean Manufacturing ultimately means nothing more than avoiding waste and delivering the products the customer wants. There are various techniques that we will briefly explain later because they can also be used in management.

3. Lean Philosophy

The success of lean manufacturing has extended the principle to many other areas, such as corporate management, accounting, maintenance and business processes in general. Corporate management is all about learning to look at your company from two perspectives:

- The customer's point of view and desires

- The company's vision and ambition to be profitable

Both perspectives have equal importance and will only lead to success if they are combined. Strict customer orientation is the most difficult task for many managers: you will have to learn to adapt your products to the customer's needs, not only in terms of quality but also in terms of price and availability. This is not so much a task in the production processes because it is a task in the setup of the company. Too often, companies are so convinced of their products that they forget what the customer wants. Incidentally, this does not contradict approaches by Apple or some start-ups that have developed products and services for which there has been no demand because they do not exist. Demand is not the same as need, rather needs create demand. Whoever creates products and services that satisfy a demand will also find a market and thus also make profits.

Dominique Keith of Dr. Kraus & Partner, in a specialist article for business-wissen.de, described very well what importance philosophy and its acceptance in management have:

The American Mike Rother, a guru of the lean scene and author of the book *The Kata of the World Market Leader: Toyota's Methods of Success*, describes the connection between lean tools or methods and Lean Management with an iceberg analogy. Lean tools and methods represent the visible part of the iceberg and Lean Management the larger, invisible part of the iceberg that is below the water surface. Many companies either completely disregard the invisible part of the iceberg when introducing a lean program or reschedule its processing.

They forget that the lean philosophy is all about a willingness to fundamentally rethink and, if necessary, change behaviors and thus bring about a fundamental cultural change in the company. The "less is more" often quoted in connection with "Lean" can also be interpreted as meaning that it is not so much about the tools but rather about the right attitude, in order to apply Lean Management and Lean Production permanently and successfully in companies.[2]

When companies restructure, they like to look at the tools, a new software, a new arrangement of desks, but less at the culture and the spirit behind it. But you'll easily find that this can't work without a change in minds. For many managers, this is the biggest challenge of lean because they also have to change their way of thinking and to a large extent their way of working. In addition, Lean needs a lot of self-reflection and you have to admit that there are mistakes and room for improvement.

3.1 Basics of Lean Management

In the past, the CEO was usually blamed and replaced when a company got into trouble—without knowing exactly what role he or she played. Today, in most cases, you're one step ahead, realizing that problems are in the nature of a business and the challenge is to identify them early enough and have appropriate methods

---

[2] Keith, D.: Schlanke Unternehmen – Was Lean Management für die Mitarbeiter bedeutet. URL: https://www.business-wissen.de/artikel/schlanke-unternehmen-was-lean-management-fuer-die-mitarbeiter-bedeutet/ [Date of Reference: 10-12-2018]

available to fix them. Things like the internal suggestion scheme already existed in Germany 30 years ago, but it was often intended to be a photo shoot for the employee magazine and employee motivation, rather than to change processes sustainably. For a long time, CEOs were afraid of change, especially when business was booming. Today, it is undisputed that only those companies that are able to quickly adapt to all changes and adjust themselves can survive.

> One **example** is the **Rügenwalder Teewurst**, one of the most famous sausages in Germany. The company producing it recognized early on that consumers increasingly want vegan products—not always, not all, but increasingly. So, the owner, Christian Rauffus, decided on something unprecedented: he began to produce vegan sausages in addition to those containing meat and launched a gigantic advertising campaign. His success proved him right: Rügenwalder Mühle is today one of the largest producers of vegan sausages in Germany.[3]

---

[3] Kolf, F. (2016): Rügenwalder Mühler, Meica, Herta – Es geht um die fleischlose Wurst. URL:
https://www.handelsblatt.com/unternehmen/handel-konsumgueter/ruegenwalder-muehle-meica-herta-es-geht-um-die-fleischlose-wurst/14448496.html [Date of Reference: 07-12-2018]

In Lean Management, you will always come across three cornerstones that form the framework: The **four principles** that a company must internalize, a **good management team** willing to accept and implement change, and a **culture** where mistakes are identified and corrected.

3.2 The Four Principles

Most literature speaks of the four basic principles of Lean Management, although some even add a fifth and even the four principles are not accepted by all experts. However, the following have proven to be particularly successful and are used accordingly in most projects and companies that have implemented Lean Management. In a much-acclaimed McKinsey study, these four principles have been seen as one of the main reasons why companies are successful with Lean Management.

1. Efficiently deliver real value to customers

Companies need to be able to better understand what customers want, when and where they want it, how they want it and why they want it. They have been resting on their sales success for too long, forgetting to ask their customers and above all to understand them. If these questions are answered, a company will be faced with the task of finding out exactly how it can deliver this benefit, no more and no less. This is where you will find the biggest challenges if you want to introduce lean because in many cases it means that you have to be self-critical. It's not about how many reviews you have, your product or your service, but about whether you *really* understand what your customers want. Neither is there a point at which everything is understood and you can keep going. It is an ongoing, never-ending process because the wishes and needs of your customers change as well.

Customer orientation is not only a task of marketing or product development but also the heart of Lean. **An example** from Switzerland, namely the **Glattpark medical** practice, shows how this customer orientation can also be reflected in small organizations such as medical practices and how processes can be optimised with it:

> "In Lean-Management-led operations, not only practitioners are "customer"-oriented, but above all the processes. The processes focus on the patient and not on the availability of resources. Conventional medical practices have fixed room allocations (waiting room, consulting room, ECG room,

blood collection room, etc.). This allocation leads to bottlenecks when a room is occupied and means unnecessary movements and changing rooms for patients. This is particularly difficult for visually impaired patients. With us, all medical activities are consistently carried out in a treatment room, which the patient enters immediately after arriving at the clinic and leaves again with the necessary information (incl. follow-up appointment etc.). All actions on the patient are performed in this room (service comes to the patient). This comfort is very much appreciated by the patients."[4]

---

[4] Bagattini, M. F. (2017): Lean Management – auch in der Arztpraxis von Vorteil! URL: https://saez.ch/de/article/doi/saez.2017.05199 [Date of Reference: 16-12-2018]

2. Encourage employees

The definition of work today is different from that of 20 years ago. It is not assigned, but employees are qualified enough to know what needs to be done but only in an environment where employees can develop, where they can work according to their qualifications and knowledge, become efficient and profitable. The task of the company is no longer to tell employees what to do but to support and encourage them in their work and to offer them the best working conditions and an appropriate environment.

This applies to all aspects of a company, from the gate-keeper to the CEO. Training alone is not enough; it's about taking the needs of employees as seriously as those of customers and responding to them. As a result, this could be, for example, a new office design, home office offers or new software requested by the employees.

3. Discover new ways to improve

The phrase "It's going well" is often heard in companies, and, as gratifying as that is, it doesn't mean that there is no potential for improvement. And that's why management in particular has to be constantly on the lookout for optimizations and improvements. The prerequisite is, of course, that one has knowledge of all areas of the organization and establishes a culture in which weak points are immediately identified. However, improvement is not an end in itself and should not be used as a buzzword. It is necessary to convey a clear idea of what "better" means. Those who understand that improvements in their own workplace are part of their daily work will help to move the company forward and continuously approach the objectives set out for them in the mission statement.

4. Combine goals, mission and strategy

When the team knows where they are going, they are ready to get involved. What used to be true especially for the explorers of the world like Columbus and Magellan is still important for companies today. If your employees know what the company's vision is, what its goals are, and what strategy should be used to achieve them, then they are more motivated to take part in this project. And motivated employees who put their hearts into it are also more efficient. Those who understand the overall picture understand their role better and are also in a better position to submit to the big picture. But that doesn't mean that you should be giving orders. Rather, it is a matter of your employees sometimes putting their needs before those of the company. Ultimately, it is a question of transparency: The more openly strategy, vision and mission are communicated and the more clearly they are laid down by the management, the stronger they are anchored in the consciousness of the employees.

David Jacquemont of McKinsey's Paris office describes the effect of the four principles on a company as follows: "As a company's experience with a new system grows, so do its resources." At the same time, Lean Management also promotes a culture in which people constantly re-evaluate themselves. Step by step, this will extend to the system itself—the company will also try to improve its implementation of Lean Management itself and consider how it can develop more ideas and go further.[5]

If you read these principles, you will surely notice that some statements also apply to your company or to companies in which you have worked before. Everybody wants to satisfy customers' needs, encourage employees, seek improvement and have a strategy. The difference, however, is that these four principles are the foundation of all activities. They are not discussed at the kick-off meeting once a year or written down in the annual report. They are lived every day by all employees. It is not only the job of market research to understand customers, and it is not only the job of human resources to support employees.

Richard Hemsley as COO has introduced Lean Management at the Royal Bank of Scotland, not an easy task considering that he has to reach 30,000 employees at the end of the day. His most important observation was that Lean is not a project that comes to an end at some

---

[5] McKinsey (2011): *Lean Management – New frontiers for financial institutions*, p. 15

point but the beginning of a process: "Compared to previous attempts at continuous improvement, the biggest difference was the investment we made in training, development and continuing Lean after the end of the implementation phase. Previously we had short-term successes in productivity or quality, but we didn't give ourselves the opportunity to evolve and take advantage of those benefits in the future. This time we have paid more attention to this aspect."[6]

---

[6] McKinsey (2011): *Lean Management – New frontiers for financial institutions*, S. 12

3.3 The Team

Any change in an organization can only be implemented if the right people are brought together to manage and execute such a project. If you want to start a lean project in your company, then it is important that there are employees from all areas in the team, especially from all management levels. A project group, which is made up of department heads and headed by the managing director, is doomed to failure because it is highly probable that only what the boss wants to hear will be said, although traditionally the middle management does not have all the necessary information. The team will have to be robust because many of the suggestions it will make will not instantly generate enthusiasm. You can apply the basic methods of change management when it comes to implementation.

Nevertheless, there are some content-related challenges for the team because even if the **four principles** are understood by all, often the trouble is in the details.

3.3.1 Principle 1: How to Understand Benefits

A CEO will define customer value differently from a salesperson in a store. There is rarely a common understanding, and it is normal for customer value to be formulated by the company and not by the customers themselves.

An **example** is a conference organized in Asia to train young people in civil society and technology. The organizers had an agenda to promote the open society through open data exchange. The conference was paid for by sponsoring organizations, which also had different agendas and set the main themes for the conference. Then suitable speakers were selected to meet the requirements of the sponsors and organizers. At no time were the participants asked what they actually wanted. And so, although many registered because it was free, in many cases they were helpless because they did not understand what the presentations were about.

Understanding and formulating customer value is, and will always be, one of the most important processes in Lean Management. At the beginning of a lean project, however, it is important to agree on a common vision. If it is difficult to reach an agreement, you can do the following:

1. Ask your salespeople, who deal most with the customers, what they think.

2. Ask customers (personally, not in a survey) about their wishes and needs.

3. If it's about introducing new products or services, then test as early as possible with a selected clientele.

3.2.2 Principle 2: What Is the Source of Waste?

If you ask your manager (or if you are yourself, yourself) where there is waste, you will find few examples. But if you ask employees who work on-site, they will be able to give you a whole list of examples. The employees "outside", as it is often called in the corporate headquarters, often have a better picture of how to improve the day-to-day business than the top managers.

Suggestions for improvement and waste are everywhere, and employees feel motivated when they see their ideas and advice being accepted and implemented. A Lean team should therefore leave the conference room as early as possible to look at day-to-day business and talk to as many employees as possible. By the way, meetings are a classic waste, especially if they are not prepared.

> **TIP:**
> In order to organize a meeting efficiently, reports should not be submitted there but only discussed. Each participant should have all the necessary documentation beforehand. This avoids long (and boring) presentations and creates time to develop more efficient solutions.

One of the best examples of how to reduce waste in wholesale and retail is the American supermarket chain **Walmart**. In retailing, one of the biggest problems is logistics: you get goods from suppliers, store them in regional centers, and then distribute them to stores that have smaller warehouses. Walmart saw a huge waste in the warehouses and created the cross-docking system.[7] This is the principle of direct delivery: a supplier brings his goods directly to the truck or railway car. The trucks unload their goods directly at the branches, where they immediately reach the shelves. This means that only small storage capacities are required.

---

[7] Soni, P. (2015): Managing Walmart's Supply Chain – Cross-Docking and Other Tools. URL: https://marketreal-ist.com/2015/02/managing-walmarts-supply-chain-cross-docking-tools [Date of Reference: 17-11-2018]

This also means that the truck fleet is constantly on the move and fewer empty runs are made.

But such a radical approach is not possible without improving planning, and Walmart invested large sums of money in its software to manage inventory and suppliers. At the same time, long-term contracts were signed with suppliers, which meant they were willing to produce according to demand rather than sell as much as possible over a short period. Another example of how to reduce waste by investing was the aggressive expansion of subsidiaries. Several experts had wondered why Walmart opened a new market when there was already a market in the area. They predicted cannibalization effects that would eventually make both stores unprofitable. But the reverse was true: one reason for the expansion was that a new store would simply establish more checkouts in an already profitable area. Customers had to wait for less time and the shopping experience was better, which ultimately resulted in both stores getting more customers.

3.2.3 Principle 3: Establish Pull

What actually comes from lean production should also be used within a team: The pull principle. Digital Kanban boards or whiteboards can help your team not to get bogged down. Just as there is waste in production and day-to-day work in a company, your lean team is no exception. So, it's important not to handle too many tasks at the same time. By taking only as many tasks from a list as can be processed simultaneously, the team itself learns how to apply lean techniques. Excessive self-testing is one of the big problems with teams that are highly motivated when it comes to change.

A good example of how to integrate Pull into the complete process is the fashion label Zara. In the company, lean has been established in all areas, but one of the biggest effects is the low storage costs. To achieve this, its founder Amancio Ortega Gaona had to come up with something special. Previously, the fashion industry had two collections a year, designed in the headquarters, and then they sent the designs to Asia, where the designs were produced in large factories and then shipped. Gaona changed this system; what mattered to him was what the customers wanted. He developed a small collection that was then tested in stores. So, Zara quickly knew what customers wanted and could produce similar designs. Today, 1,000 different garments are designed, produced and sold every month. The company keeps a close eye on how long a customer stays in a store and what he or she buys and reacts immediately when there are changes.

Zara has also introduced and perfected just-in-time production in the fashion industry. Instead of producing everything in Asia, where you have lower wages but also high production costs and expenses for quality management, Zara produces in 300 factories in North Africa and Turkey. This makes it possible to bring products to the European market within 24 hours and to North America and Asia in 40 hours.

This makes the company four times more profitable than other competitors. Only those products that can be sold quickly are produced. If a T-shirt, gown or suit is sold, it is either reproduced or a new design with similar characteristics is brought into the shops. The customer orientation goes so far that every day after closing time the managers in the 2,000 stores in 88 countries sit down at their computer and enter what they have learned about the customers and their buying behavior on that day. This data goes directly to the designers' headquarters, who then create the new designs based on it. All returned goods and the reasons for the return are also recorded.

3.2.4 Principle 4: Continuous Team Improvement

The group that is responsible for implementing Lean Management should also be able to constantly improve itself. As a team leader, you will need to make sure that you don't get stuck in a project plan but have methods to reflect on your own work. This can be done through key figures that are established for the employees and the project progress or through milestones that are jointly formulated. The employees should not be over-taxed because an old saying goes, "Multitasking is the best way to do more than one thing wrong at the same time."

If you have understood the **four basic principles** of Lean Management and know what role your team plays in the introduction of Lean, then you can venture into the topic of culture.

3.4 A Culture That Solves Problems

The success of change always depends on the culture of the company. Culture evolves and cannot be decreed from above. But you can at least guide this development in certain directions if you are aware of it. There is no real corporate culture but only one that has grown in a certain company and largely determines the everyday lives of its employees.

Organizations that have an open culture, in which something new is accepted, have it easier to change than those that have very rigid structures. Łukasz Dekier, in a paper on the origins and evolution of Lean Management, identified a number of factors that define a culture in which Lean Management can be best developed.

3.4.1 A Good Atmosphere at the Workplace

It is essential that the employer ensures that there is a good working atmosphere. This does not only help the employees to do their work but also builds bridges between employees and the company. As a result, employees are more motivated, even if, for example, they have to work overtime one day because of the work required—and this work is done with the same quality during overtime.

3.4.2 Setting Clear Objectives

For someone to do a good job, he or she needs to know what the common goal is and what his or her goal is. To make this clear, there must be short-term as well as medium- and long-term goals for the employee. Practically, this means that he or she must see a future in the company, for example about career opportunities, but also what needs to be done in day-to-day work must be very clear. In a company that works according to the Lean Management System, career paths are also transparent and employees know the requirements they need, for example, to be promoted.

3.4.3 Communication

Whenever there are problems in a company, often you will find the cause in a lack of communication, especially in the area of personnel development. In a Lean system there are no communication barriers, rather it is required that you communicate with each other across department heads and hierarchical levels. "It's not my task," or, "I am overqualified for it," are not statements that are helpful in such an environment. Short day meetings that briefly clarify where there are problems and how they can be solved can be of help. This brings together all those who are active in a particular area—as long as it makes sense considering the size of the group. It is important that not (only) a team leader or a department manager speaks but that the employees have their say and can decide during the meeting. In the area of software development, the daily stand-ups have such a function, although they concentrate more on the actual production. But if you already have experience with Scrum and Agile, you will have experienced such meetings and can easily implement them in other industries.

3.4.4 The Right Motivation

In Lean Management, managers are asked to leave the traditional reward and motivation systems behind. Instead of salary increases and the old carrot-and-stick system, new ways are needed to motivate employees because the disadvantage of the classic rewards is that they usually only have a short-term effect and only motivate employees for the reward but not to advance the company. Better motivations are clear career opportunities, as mentioned above, but also improvements in the working environment, such as the possibility to work partly from home, if family circumstances permit. The most important thing, however, is to transfer responsibility to the employees. Nothing motivates as much as the trust you get when you want to be responsible for a task. In Lean Management, it is therefore particularly important for managers to be able to give up control.

3.4.5 Do Not Waste Your Own Personnel Capacities

Often, when an organization is operating successfully for a long time and the business figures are also good, the development of the personnel is neglected. After all, everyone does their job. However, in many cases their full potential is not exploited and valuable personnel resources are wasted.

EXAMPLE:

An accounting employee who has been with a company for 15 years knows the balance sheets and accounts inside out and has undergone several restructurings. He has clear tasks but few new challenges. During his spare time, he started working with FinTech, which had to deal with mobile transactions, which was not yet in use in their own company. He shares his ideas with his supervisor, who simply says that he will pass them on to his IT colleagues.

The only problem is that IT has no skills when it comes to the strategic evaluation of mobile transactions. Nobody in the company has them, except the employee who raised the issue. It would be a waste to bring him back to his desk and hire external staff to set up the project. Instead, you should give the employee at least one role in the project or—depending on their skills—even let them lead the project.

3.4.6 Allow Employees to Develop Themselves

It is in our human nature that we are curious and like to discover new things, even if we become lazier with age. People working for a company today want more than just a desk and a monthly salary. Today, employees are highly qualified in almost all areas. Even a car mechanic is no longer the first to pick up a wrench when inspecting a car but connects the diagnostic device to the vehicle's electronics. If you don't constantly train your employees in a car company, they will either no longer be able to repair a car or move to other companies that offer them better training opportunities. With lean companies, it's not a waste to invest in training because you don't exploit the full potential of existing employees.

For managers, it is above all the so-called soft skills that need to be developed. The background is that people are only motivated if they have a competent motivator. In a modern company, employees follow management because they want to and not because they have to. But this can only be achieved by leaders who are resilient, who have professional competencies, who can give up control, who can control and reflect on themselves, and above all who are capable of both living a vision themselves and communicating it to others.

3.4.7 Hoshin Kanri

Also, in this case, the Japanese have developed a method that tries to implement the visions of a company in such a way that they are ultimately reflected in the culture. Hoshin Kanri means "management's compass needle" and serves to transfer the corporate vision to all other levels of the company in order to align activities with overarching goals and continuous learning, as well as the improvement of processes. The systematic communication between the company levels and between the functional areas leads to a target-oriented planning of processes and activities as well as existing improvement potentials. Possible conflicts of objectives between company levels or areas are prevented by better communication.[8]

A culture of continuous improvement can only develop if an organization is able to learn and has a common language. In Hoshin Kanri, the strategic goals are broken

---

[8] Busse, M. (2017): *Implementing Lean Management – ein ganzheitliches Vorgehensmodell zur nachhaltigen Implementierung des Lean Managements in KMU*, p. 78

down by the management into sub-goals, which are then passed on to middle management. These are then used to derive operational measures at the lower levels. The important thing is that a solution is not found to problems at the lower level but that the problem is discussed together with the upper levels.

The advantage of the Hoshin method is that visions and strategies are communicated down to the last detail. However, one of the disadvantages is the top-down approach: The lower levels only have the execution and this can have a demotivating effect. In addition, it can occur that too many small goals are to be achieved at the same time. This can be compensated by a catchball system where there are regular meetings where the opinions of employees at all levels are solicited. Hoshin has a tendency to quickly become too bureaucratic and to place strategic goals above day-to-day goals.

The name Catchball comes from the idea that the management formulates the strategies and visions then throws these ideas to the lower levels like a ball and waits for feedback.

4. Lean Management Methods

There are several methods that are closely linked to lean production and Lean Management and also express the underlying philosophy. You can use these methods individually or in combination. They all come from production but have been generalised and can now be used in management and corporate governance.

4.1 Kaizen

This Japanese principle says that there is constant improvement. It means change for the better, which already tells you that it is positive: Change is good and not an end in itself. Kaizen improvement is a continuous process that never ends. It takes place on all levels. Often such improvements are only small details, but they can have a big impact. To a certain extent, this contradicts the innovation that is usually made at certain intervals. In Kaizen, a product, a company or a service is constantly improved and changed.

This has been incorporated into the theory of the Continuous Improvement Process (CIP) in Western management. It includes:

- Internal suggestion scheme

- Further training

- Process orientation

- Reduction of hierarchy levels

- Quality management and management

The disadvantage of this constant improvement, however, is that only existing products and services are used, and some of them grow into monsters that are difficult to manage. One example is web agencies that offer software development, develop apps and specialize in virtual reality. There may come a point where it is better not to further develop a product or service but to divide it into several components. Nevertheless, the basic attitude of never resting and always looking for improvement is an essential part of Lean Management.

4.2 Kaikaku

The philosophy of Kaikaku is the exact opposite of Kaizen and means radical change. The original philosophy was that a company must be able to fundamentally change certain production processes at least for a certain period. While Kaizen is a continuous process, Kaikaku has a short life span and is usually introduced as a project. Therefore, it is not so much a corporate philosophy but a method to quickly and effectively implement changes. The Japanese Hiroyuki Hirano, who also developed the 5S method, describes the 10 basic rules of Kaikaku[9] as follows:

- Throw all traditional production methods overboard

- Imagine how the new method works, not how it doesn't work

- Don't accept excuses. Deny the status quo

- Don't look for perfection. A 50% implementation is fine as long as it is done immediately

- Improve errors as soon as you find them

---

[9] Kaizenworld (2016): Kaikaku. URL:
https://www.kaizenworld.com/kaizen-blog/kaikaku.html [Date of Reference: 21-11-2018]

- Don't spend money on Kaikaku

- A problem is a chance to use your brain

- Answer the Five "Why"

- The ideas of ten people are more valuable than the knowledge of one person

- Kaikaku knows no boundaries

Though Kaikaku is perceived as radical, its implementation is less radical. Or in other words: the radical approach helps to really get a change going. But it won't be possible to keep up the pace for long, and that's why Kaikaku is such a good complement to Kaizen. It is usually the initial spark that sets new processes in motion or forces management to change course right away.

4.3 Kanban

Kanban is actually a method that comes from production control. It is based on the actual demand for raw materials and production resources, as well as materials at the production location. It is an essential part of just-in-time production and helps to reduce inventories and also prevent products from being thrown away because the shelf life in the warehouse has expired (for example, in the pharmaceutical industry). It works with cards that track the materials used. In the production control, boards are used on which the work is recorded. They are divided into To Do, Doing and Done (in the simplest form) and have a maximum capacity. This ensures that the system only does as much work as it can handle.

Nevertheless, Kanban has been in project management for a long time now, where it offers a good overview of how good the workflow is and whether there are any problems that might arise when the workflow stops. In management, Kanban is used to achieve a work flow that is as uniform as possible so that no resources are wasted. As with all lean methods, errors are quickly detected and corrected to restore the flow.

Wikipedia emphasizes the importance of workflow: "One of the most important design principles of lean management is the continuous and smooth flow of production, the flow principle. In many organizations, departmental boundaries are optimised, lines and cells are run at maximum productivity, but this function-oriented way of thinking does not necessarily lead to the optimum. If you look at the production process from the product point of view, you can see the many stops in the form of temporary storage and buffer stocks."[10]

4.4 Six Sigma

Six Sigma was introduced by Motorola in the USA in the late '70s to improve production. It is a management system designed to improve processes, work with data, and be a tool for quality improvement. At its core, business processes are examined with data and improved on the basis of the resulting analyses. The method is based on five elements:

- Define

---

[10] riss Consulting (2016): Qualitätsmanagement. URL: http://www.riss.de/consulting/qualitaetsmanagement/ [Date of Reference: 24-11-2018]

- Measure

- Analyze

- Improve

- Control

The principle was soon adopted by Jack Welch, the powerful CEO of General Electric, and eventually became a standard in the manufacturing industry. But many service companies also use this method. It is also widespread because it provides facts that are easier to evaluate than just a philosophy. In a Six Sigma project, roles are assigned according to the belt colors of Japanese martial arts. There is the champion, the black master belt (coach and trainer), the black belt (full-time in the project with high competence) and green belt (management, mostly department heads). The colors white, yellow and blue are also used but not for project management tasks.

Six Sigma is therefore part of Lean Management and Lean Manufacturing because it aims at constantly improving processes and thus achieves savings where resources are being wasted.

4.5 5S

A very well-known and simple method from the area of Lean Management and Lean Production is the 5S system, which also originates from Toyota. The five S's stand for:

"Seiri

Sort it out. Anything that is not needed to work at this location should be sorted out."

"Seiton

Put it up neatly. What is actually needed is ergonomically selected, defined and assigned a fixed location."

"Seiso

Clean. Everyone cleans their own workplace and working tools. Defects are detected, marked and constantly processed. The cleaning helps to check."

"Seiketsu

Standardize. This means that uniform markings, inscriptions and markings can be used throughout the entire workplace at all times. Constant tidying up prevents new objects from being brought into the workplace unplanned."

"Shitsuke

Self-discipline and continuous improvement (Kaizen). Discipline is required to maintain order and cleanliness. Once a tool's storage space has been defined, it should always be there. Regular checks are carried out and irregularities are noted. Any irregularities found must be rectified."[11]

In a more general sense, what initially applied to jobs in production is increasingly being implemented in other areas as well. This means that almost all processes in a company can be optimized.

5S is only made up of a few elements, which is why it can be regarded as uncomplicated. The continuous maintenance of order on the one hand increases the time required for the application of this method; on the other hand, the order created during the first run and its standards lead to faster processing of further runs. From an SME perspective, the short duration of training

---

[11] detektierbar.de (2016): 5S Sortiment – Lean Management. URL: https://detektierbar.de/5s-sortiment.html [Date of Reference: 27-12-2018]

and the short time required for its application in the company are positive aspects. The benefit of 5S lies in the reduction of throughput time, which can be achieved by avoiding search times, the disclosure of improvement potentials and the increase in the well-being of the employees at the workplace. By integrating the employees in the workplace design in connection with the avoidance of waste, employee motivation is increased. [12]

For example, in a service company, 5S can be used to organize desks, especially in shared offices. Here are some examples of what you can avoid:

- Information overload

- No need to move documents

- Long walks of employees

- Waiting for feedback/releases

- Inappropriate IT systems

- Suboptimal storage/archiving

- Wasteful activities

---

[12] Busse, M. (2017): *Implementing Lean Management – ein ganzheitliches Vorgehensmodell zur nachhaltigen Implementierung des Lean Managements in KMU*, p. 78

- Superfluous queries

- Unreadable data formats/documents

- Obsolete documents

The 5S method can be applied on its own, in order to obtain quick results, or it can be integrated into other methods mentioned above. For example, the last S is an essential part of Kaizen. The 5S are also well suited to be used as a pilot project and as a cautious introduction to Lean Management because they are very clearly comprehensible. The advantages of a proper archive are clear to everyone, as well as the fact that the coffee kitchen is tidy and everyone knows where the sugar is.

But as a manager it will be important that you also internalize and practice these methods. 5S should be developed as a basic principle for an entire organization; only the specific applications will be different. Since it is so easy to understand, it is also a good idea for you to introduce the principle from the management side, but leave it up to the individual departments to decide how to implement it.

With 5S you will get a better grip on the sloppiness and carelessness that arise in every small company over time.

Examples are:

- Wastage of ballpoint pens: If you can't find your pen, a new one will simply be taken out of stock.

- Unlabeled files: Nobody knows what was filed, and if it is a contract from 2014, you will waste a lot of time looking for it.

- Moving boxes: The company moved four years ago and yet there are still boxes that haven't been unpacked. Either the contents are no longer needed, in which case they can be removed and space created, or they are taken to the right place.

- Office supplies: Companies waste huge sums of money on office supplies such as paper clips, markers, tapes and others. A clearly organized warehouse helps in saving a lot of money.

- Mobile phone bills: If your company uses land-lines, it will be expensive to call someone on a mobile phone just because you're away from your desk. A clear rule can also save costs here.

- Electricity bills: Letting the coffee machine heat all day is just as wasteful as not turning off the lights in the conference room, not shutting down the computer when you leave your desk for a long time, or not closing a window in winter.

This may all sound trivial, but it's a quicker way to realize the importance of lean and the fight against waste, rather than having a staff of consultants to give a four-day seminar on the Toyota production system.

4.6 5 Why

The Five Why or Why's method is part of Lean Management and also comes from production. It's about really getting to the bottom of a problem. At least five questions are asked about what happened.

Example: Program crashed when using older Android versions

Why?

Because we didn't test all versions.

Why?

Because it wasn't in the job description.

Why?

Because the budget doesn't allow us to test old versions.

Why?

Because we didn't include it in the project description.

Why?

Because the time frame of the project would not have been sufficient.

This is not a simple bug to fix but a systematic bug. In such a case you would try to find out things that couldn't be done for budget reasons but could be critical for the software.

In an environment where there's a constant need for improvement, this is only possible if you know the real problems and make improvements where they have the greatest effect. The 5W method can also help to identify such areas. 5W was also developed by Sackicho Toyoda for Toyota production. This also gave a more scientific claim to new ideas because you had to do more research to find causes.

By the way, it turned out that such analyses are best carried out in a group and with a blackboard, rather than everybody working individually on their own computer. And you will notice that the chains of questions can take different directions because, for example, you get two answers for the same question. In this case you can follow both paths. But always remember that the point is to find the causes and not to describe symptoms. Work your way up to the problem step by step. Don't try to get straight to the root cause. Another advice is to always focus on processes, not on people. If an employee has made a mistake, this is regrettable, but he will notice it himself. Rather, the question is can something be improved in the process to minimize such human errors? In an ideal form of Lean Management, you will go through the 5W process from the customer's point of view, especially when it comes to why questions.

4.6 Other Methods

There are innumerable methods and methods that are used as tools in Lean Management and Lean Production. A prime example is **McDonald's**, which has extremely internalized the basic principles of Lean and even invented its own methods, the Speedy system.

> The founders of McDonald's quickly recognized one of the biggest problems with burger restaurants: waiting time. Much of the waiting time for the customer and the time used in production was caused by the operation: one person did it all alone. That was changed: In the Speedy system, there is a kind of assembly line along which the burger is assembled. This may look like excess staff for an order, but it turned out to be a major advantage when compared to the many orders the stores had.

> However, the managers at the fast food chain did not stop improving. It turned out that the customers didn't want hamburgers that were kept warm, even if they were only under the heat lamp for a certain time. Pre-production had the advantage of always having a certain amount of the best-selling

products ready, thereby reducing the waiting time. However, many burgers also had to be thrown away because they were kept warm for too long. This had an impact on the production process: McDonald's now uses just-in-time production, where the ingredients are already prepared in such a way that in the end only the meat has to be grilled, this way the burger still reaches the tray quickly.

Waiting times have also been significantly reduced by incorporating technology: once an order is completed at the checkout, it reaches the kitchen, which then processes the order in less than three minutes.[13]

---

[13] Mrunal (2014): Lean Production at McDonalds. URL: http://cmuscm.blogspot.com/2014/09/lean-production-at-mcdonalds.html [Date of Reference: 28-10-2018]

5. When and Where Can Lean Be Used?

Lean production originated from large companies such as Toyota and General Electric. There, the savings potential was great, many structures were encrusted and internal innovation was not really promoted. Lean was initially used in production precisely because small savings combined with large volumes also have large effects. Small and medium-sized companies have long been of the opinion that they are lean in themselves.

But since lean can also be applied to management and services, SMEs have also woken up. Nevertheless, these companies are the engines of innovation in many areas today. "Large European companies naturally have an advantage when it comes to labour productivity (59,000 euros compared to 39,000 euros for SMEs per employee). But the productivity gap is closing more and more because even smaller companies are beginning to make production more cost-effective. Today SMEs are the driving force of the modern economy, because they use new technologies, develop new products and invent new processes", states Tamara Tsõgankova in her master thesis on Lean Management in SMEs in Estonia.[14]

One reason is the new calculation formula for profits. This definition has been used for a long time:
Profit = Price - Costs

That has changed today. The new formula is:
Profit = (Price - Costs) x Volume

The difference is that for a long time people tried to reduce costs in order to increase profit, but today they understand that increasing volume can have a greater effect.

When a company is in crisis, the first thing they often do is lay off employees. Although this relieves the balance sheets in the short term, it does not generate any new income. It therefore makes more sense to check how you can make more sales with existing employees. For a company that is completely over-indebted, lean usually comes too late because it takes some time for it to unfold its full potential. For example, if there are early signs of an impending crisis, Lean can be used to turn the tide.

---

[14] Tsõgankova, T. (2014): *Lean Implementation in Estonian SMEs based on the example of the company Narva Tes Plus*

Lean is useful for SMEs if …

- … productivity figures are falling

- … an organization has not changed over a long period

- … a company wants to become more resilient

- … new forms of employee motivation are needed because otherwise they will migrate

- … cost savings do not bring the desired effect

The following can be achieved with Lean Management in SMEs:

- Increase in productivity

- Shorter lead times

- Reduce material and inventory levels

- Reduce production costs

- Motivate employees

- Reduce fluctuation figures

- Improve the skills and abilities of employees

- Establish and promote knowledge management

- Increase flexibility

- Strengthen employee loyalty

- Increase customer satisfaction

- Improve collaboration with partners

- Improve your position in the financial market

- Create/improve confidence between other market participants

The above points should not in fact raise doubts as to whether Lean can also be applied to small and medium-sized enterprises.

However, SMEs also have a certain risk potential when it comes to implementing Lean Management. One problem is the lack of resources, especially in terms of personnel. In small companies, it is very difficult to put together a project team that can spend a lot of time on a Lean Project. In addition, there is simply a lack of knowledge: Many SMEs have to purchase external consultants who first explain what Lean Management is all about. Such costs are long-term investments that often do not seem to be compatible with short-term day-to-day business.

Another problem is that many employees are very specialized in following the traditional management model. They have very narrow areas of responsibility. Even in middle management and sometimes at the very top, there is a lack of new knowledge about modern company management. Family and owner-managed companies are particularly vulnerable. This often leads to decisions being made intuitively.

SMEs also traditionally have structural weaknesses that usually start at the top. Managing directors and owners tend to neglect guiding and strategic work and instead deal with organization and problem solving, which is actually the task of middle management. Thereby, their work is shifted into the operative day-to-day business in which they do not have the necessary competences. This then leads to friction losses at the so-called shop floor level, which can have major effects. Unsatisfied employees quickly and frequently fall ill and are more likely to look for a new job and generally perform worse.

EXAMPLE:

In a PR agency near Frankfurt, the owner's good contacts helped to win many orders. This led to the fact that he also looked after his client at least partially after the conclusion of a contract. The key account employee, who was actually supposed to lead the campaign, was increasingly driven into the area of measures and then had to organize events, which he could not do. The employees at the events were confused, there was no well-formulated plan and a press conference failed because the employee had used the wrong press distribution list. However, it was just as bad that the owner no longer did strategic work but devoted himself almost exclusively to acquisition. In the end, this led to the company having a technological disadvantage—the owner had simply misjudged the possibilities of the emerging Internet and dismissed it as a gimmick.

W.J. Gartner describes the problem in his management book[15] as follows: "The owner-entrepreneur unit is disadvantageous if the entrepreneur adopts an authoritarian management style. The separation of the decisive and the executive person leads to a distanced relationship between the employees and the executive. The employees are demotivated and refuse to act on their own initiative and to get involved in problems."

---

[15] Gartner, W. J. (2002): *Management - Einführung in Managament, Kommunikation und Personalwirtschaft, Oldenbourg Wissenschaftsverlag GmbH*, p. 260 sq.

6. Management Requirements

In addition to the fundamental willingness to change a company, there are a number of other requirements to be met by the management and the organization so that Lean can be successfully implemented.

6.1 Cost

One of the uncertainties that comes with Lean is the estimation of costs. Lean, like many other restructuring projects, is not as easy to quantify as the introduction of a new production line or the purchase of new accounting software. This is often one of the reasons why management hesitates, especially when shareholders ask what the ROI is, when Lean is introduced. However, this can be quantified at least theoretically, if you introduce key figures that are to be achieved.

> **EXAMPLE:**
> If you want to introduce Lean because you want to improve your sales force, you can of course express this desired improvement in figures, for ex-

ample 5 percent increase in sales, 10 percent savings in transport costs, 15 percent more new customers.

6.2 Acceptance by Employees

Martin Busse describes the problems and advantages
that SMEs have with their employees when it comes to
change: "SMEs have an increased need for transparency
and a goal-oriented implementation due to the close
ties and the friendly family relationship between the
employees. The negative attitude of employees, resulting from poor information or failed implementation attempts, increases the costs of implementation and
worsens the initial situation. Employees are informed
and motivated to cooperate on the basis of comprehen-
sive information and individual communication. Existing behavioral patterns have to be successively adapted
to changed circumstances and the new management
system, while the old management system is gradually
replaced".

The special structure of SMEs, especially their proximity
to employees, can be a great advantage in change management. Especially when transparency has already

been exemplified, employees can be better motivated if there is a sense of togetherness in the company and if they have already gone through thick and thin together before.

EXAMPLE:

Kimberly Deranek and Dr. Shweta Chopra chose a company that had already established Lean for a study that looked at the success factors involved in introducing Lean. It was a Midwestern company that focused on the production of specialized products that needed a lot of engineering knowledge. The company had 200 products but less than 10 full-time employees. The two researchers accompanied the company for a year and found out, among other things, that the role of management in the process was of utmost importance. "A big success factor in the company are the executives and the management. Both showed great commitment to the employees, where they were visible and available." Several studies have shown that managers who regularly visit production sites and talk to employees about Lean and other processes motivate them much more to implement them. The way management presented itself significantly improved teamwork, adaptability and process optimisation. There was room for innovation and employees were encouraged and trained, especially beyond their actual special field. All employees had knowledge of at least three areas from within the company; two were even trained in all areas. One of the consequences of this was that every employee knew what their colleagues were capable of and how and where they could be deployed if, for example, there was a bottleneck. What particularly stood out was the high level of involvement, which in English is often referred to as ownership. The employees saw themselves as part of the company, their work was THEIR work, and they felt responsible for it.[16]

This was also made possible because the management treated the employees accordingly: with respect and friendliness, just as one behaves towards family members and good friends. Trust was another factor that could be proven when they wanted to make a difference in the factory. The construction plans were worked out together, all employees could contribute ideas for what could be improved and at the same time

---

[16] Deranek, K.; Chopra, S.; Mosher, G. A. (2017): *Lean Adoption in Small and Medium Enterprise Validation*

knew that they would actually be accepted. This went so far that the management could concentrate on the strategic aspects and the employees took over the planning and implementation.

6.3 Clear Benefits

If you work in a medium-sized company, you will already have experienced that the cost pressure is high, often the competition and always the threat of being swallowed by a large company or being driven out of the market. That is why SMEs usually have little room for experimentation. This makes it all the more important that Lean Management brings immediate benefits. Smaller companies cannot afford protracted introduction phases; sometimes they do not even have the capacity to start a pilot project in just one department. So, if you are considering introducing Lean Management, you should clearly emphasize the expected benefits.

In China, many SMEs still find it difficult to apply new methods. On the other hand, the demand for mass production is high, but the companies do not have the technical capabilities. Staufen AG advises companies internationally on Lean Management and reports on so-called flexible assembly cells, which can be easily implemented and have immediate effects: "For example, experience with a filter-producing company in Shanghai shows that the concept of the flexible assembly cell can improve production. A double U-cell was introduced, which was designed on the basis of ergonomic concepts in such a way that the entire production layout was optimised. This allowed the production line to be increased from 51% to 87%, the usable area reduced from 240 m2 to 64 m2 and productivity increased by 100%."[17]

> **EXAMPLE PRINTING HOUSE:**
>
> In a printing company specializing in the production of stickers, they wanted to introduce Lean in order to increase productivity and efficiency. One reason was that they didn't produce as many stickers as the machines could, which in turn affected

---

[17] Staufen AG (2014): Ein guter Weg um Lean Production in kleinen und mittelgroßen chinesischen Unternmehmen (SMEs) zu starten: Das Komzept der flexiblen Montagezelle. URL: https://www.staufen.ag/de/unternehmen/news-events/news/newsdetail/2014/08/ein-guter-weg-um-lean-production-in-kleinen-und-mittelgrossen-chinesischen-unternehmen-smes-zu-star/ [Date of Reference: 12-12-2018]

the time factor and therefore the price. The management went to the print shop and spoke to the printers and department heads. Everyone involved in printing was interviewed. It soon turned out that a lot of time was spent on the printing process, 115 minutes per job. The process consists of test printing, printing, die cutting, cutting, drying and packaging. However, it soon became apparent that these processes were actually running smoothly. In group discussions, it was discovered that the delays were mainly due to the setup of the machines. They took a closer look at this process and it turned out that the better the machines were set up at the beginning, the less time and material was needed for the test prints and the faster the actual printing process could begin. The process was optimised, including ink filling and plates. The result was an eight-hour shift that improved 600 hours to 5142 hours. That was an improvement of 20 percent. The time required to set up the printing machine was reduced from 51 to 35 minutes.[18]

---

[18] Rishi et al. (2018): *Implementing the Lean Framework in a Small & Medium & Enterprise (SME) – A case Study in Printing Press, IOP Publishing, IOC Conf. Ser.*, volume 376, conference 1

7. Lean Leadership

The concept of Lean Leadership is closely linked to the philosophy of Lean Management. However, it is less about streamlining management or leadership. Rather, it was the method used by Toyota to train its managers. In the Japanese company, the focus was placed very early on employees and above all on people—something that actually contradicts our stereotypes of Japanese offices. It was recognized that it is much more effective and successful to empower employees than to instruct them. Previous leadership was—and still is in many companies—always tied to instructions given from top to bottom. In the case of mistakes, the employees were held responsible (and felt responsible to a large extent). However, this did not solve the problem of why the mistake happened.

Toyota began to systematically train its employees through the Lean Leadership Development Program, especially in leadership skills. The ultimate goal was to expand competencies. The theory is that if managers become more competent, this will also help the entire organization because it will accumulate more competence and knowledge. This also meant that you had to keep an eye on the organization and not just on your own area. Managers were trained to solve problems that benefited the entire company and not just to seek partial success. This systemic approach can still be found in many companies today.

The management model focused on several steps that future managers had to go through:

Step 1: Learn to reflect on yourself

Only when you know who you are and are able to critically review your behavior will you be able to improve your own performance and that of your employees.

Step 2: Coaching

Once the process of inner reflection is complete, managers can begin to lead other managers and employees so that they can evaluate themselves. Coaching is also about making sure that the goal is to provide the organization with better and more competent employees.

Step 3: Developing groups

While in the second step you only devote yourself to individual employees, in the third step you will develop groups and teams and even entire depart-ments. The focus here is on team skills, how to work together, which optimizations are possible but also how the Kaizen philosophy can be implemented.

Step 4: Becoming a Lean Leader

In the development of an executive into a Lean Leader, the end result is a manager who can devote himself to the visions and strategies of the company. You have developed your employees so far that they can work efficiently and on their own responsibility, identify waste and take measures to eliminate it sustainably. Now you can dedicate yourself to the organization, the structures of your company and look for bottlenecks and silos. In this last step the competence of the organization itself will be improved, with new organization hierarchy flattening, new production methods and other measures.

The American Lean Consultant Lonnie Wilson[19] conducted very thorough analysis of the problems in the American management system as early as 2013. Be-

---

[19] Wilson, L. (2013): Six Qualities of Lean Leadership. URL: https://www.industryweek.com/continuous-improvement/six-qualities-lean-leadership [Date of Reference: 01-12-2018]

sides the belief in numbers, he saw the reason for Japanese companies being better managed as the belief that you can manage and lead from an office without having to contact local employees. "Therefore, machines have become pure capital that does not require management attention. Worse still was the belief that employees were ultimately only cost centres, not even capital, that could be exchanged at will." And because they were only costs, attempts were made to reduce them. Wilson sees this treatment of employees as the worst mistake of traditional management.

He came up with the **six qualities** a Lean Leader should have:

- Leaders should be able to observe and spend time with employees.

- Leaders should be able to learn and not pretend to know everything.

- Leaders should be initiators and not shy away from risk.

- Leaders should be teachers, and if something goes wrong in the company, they should consider what mistake they have made as teachers.

- Leaders are role models: They themselves do what they ask of others.

- Leaders support and understand their role as someone who empowers others to do better.

8. Lean Start-Up

In an article in the *Harvard Business Review*, Steve Blank[20] argued that Lean Management is the miracle cure for why start-ups are faster and more flexible than companies that have grown over time and have some market dominance. "Business plans rarely survive the first contact with a customer." Or, as the boxer Mike Tyson once put it when asked about his strategy, Everyone has a plan until the opponent's first hit lands on his nose. The way start-ups are managed today can also serve as a role model for existing companies.

8.1 Business Model Canvas

The young founders of companies today are less concerned with making plans for weeks and researching the market down to the last detail. Their approach is a rough idea of what they want to do, a hypothesis that is then formulated in a business model canvas.

---

[20] Blank, S. (2013): Why the Lean Start-Up Changes Everything. URL: https://hbr.org/2013/05/why-the-lean-start-up-changes-everything [Date of Reference: 13-11-2018]

It contains the following elements:

Problem:	Solution approach:		
Competition:	Main partners:	Main activities:	Customer relationships:
Main Resources:	Value Proposition:	Channels:	Customer segmentation:
Cost Structures:		Revenue:	

By filling out this table, you can see at a glance what a 50-page business plan would be. The table describes all important aspects of your business.

8.2 Customer Orientation

In a modern start-up, services are not developed until they meet the expectations of the founders. Rather, only parts of them are developed and then immediately offered to customers for testing. Part of Lean Management is to save time by obtaining customer feedback as quickly as possible and make changes at an early stage.

You don't even have to have real customers at this point. It is enough to interview potential customers, explain your product idea or service to them and ask them what their wishes and needs are.

> **EXAMPLE:**
>
> A developer of a hotel booking website who specialized in hotels in his home country suspected that he could not compete with the big global booking sites. So, he went to hotels, sat by the pool and asked hotel guests how they planned their vacation. It turned out that many travel with large families or in small groups, and it is difficult to find hotels that offer family rooms. From then on, he specialized in hotels offering such multi-bed rooms.

8.3 MVP

At this stage, start-ups also have the so-called Minimal Viable product, i.e. a product that only meets the minimum requirements and just works. Many of the big social networks started out this way, and Google was just a line of input that produced search results. Particularly in software development, there is a tendency to want too many features right from the start, which considerably prolongs the development time without knowing whether the customer really needs them. If you start with a rudimentary product, it's easier to implement customer feedback and make changes. These so-called iterations accelerate the entire development process but also save costs because you don't have to do expensive market research. But the basic requirement is that you trust and listen to your customers and take their needs seriously. You will find many examples of founders who have put too much fancy into their product and who have turned their backs on the advice and wishes of their customers.

8.4 Agile Working Environment

The term Agile actually comes from software development and describes a framework in which the software is continuously improved in small steps by the development team. These small steps allow a constant input by the customer, who is therefore directly involved in the development and not only a finished product to accept. The big advantage here is enormous time savings. Even if it is not even clear what the finished product should look like, you can already start working on it as soon as you are Agile. But Agile is more than just software development, it can also change a company's entire way of thinking and working. Elements from Scrum, a well-known Agile method in management, such as short daily briefings and sprints and two-week work cycles for specific product parts, are adopted.

You don't have to start a new company to take advantage of the start-ups, but you can run an existing company as if it were a start-up. With smaller companies this is usually possible without major problems, and you can also apply the start-up method only to certain areas, especially in product development.

> **EXAMPLE:**
>
> A company that produces wooden toys wants to boost sales with new ideas but doesn't really know where to start. One approach would be to sit in a toy shop with a play corner and see which toys the children use and how. If you get an idea, for example a modular plug-in system, you can turn it into a simple prototype that you can then give to children for testing. Children handle things differently from adults, which is why it can happen that a plug connection lasts in the company but a child breaks it after a few minutes.

8.5 Design Thinking

Particularly when it comes to prototypes, Design Thinking is an increasingly popular way to quickly develop lots of ideas. Design Thinking is a method used to solve problems in a practical and creative way. This means—unlike open brainstorming—there must be a solution to a problem at the end of the process. This problem can be a problem that actually exists or one that you believe could arise in the future.

In the process of Design Thinking you will also learn that assumptions are not always correct. One game illustrates that quite well, which you can also play with your management team or other employees.

The participants have to build the **tallest possible tower** out of **dry spaghetti noodles**, **some tape and string** and a **marshmallow**. Tom Wujec[21] invented this game to show that our assumptions are often wrong, for example that a marshmallow is very light and some spaghetti can keep it loose (it has to form the top of the tower during the game). It shows that you can't always solve problems with an analytical approach, and teams often have only one approach. The goal of the game is to build a tower with as much trial and error as possible but also to work in a team and welcome all suggestions.

---

[21] Wujec, T. (2010): Build a tower, build a team. URL: https://www.ted.com/talks/tom_wujec_build_a_tower [Date of Reference: 25-10-2018]

There are **three main processes** in Design Thinking:

Interdisciplinary

The interdisciplinary process means that a team must be permanently diverse during the different phases. Three engineers alone will achieve just as little as three graphic designers. But if you put all six together and add a few other employees, something new can emerge.

Iterative

Design Thinking is a non-linear model. There are no milestones like in project management that are processed one after the other. Instead, it is an iterative process in which you will and must go backwards repeatedly.

Flexible

In creative processes, prohibiting thinking is the worst thing that can happen. A boss who starts a Design Thinking project with the words, "Be creative, but please make sure you only use our own products, make sure the product is small so that we can ship it quickly," would have better said nothing because a design project must be goal-oriented but also open to results. This means that at the beginning you have no idea of what will actually come out at the end.

9. Success Factors and Problems in Lean Management

In order for Lean to be successfully implemented in a company, knowledge of the various factors that influence such a project is required. Busse divides these into two groups:

- General success factors

- Critical success factors

The **general factors** include, primarily, the nature of the company and its culture and orientation.

Such factors in detail include:

- Holistic nature

- Self-conception and knowledge of necessity

- Stringent goal orientation

- Long-term orientation

- Corporate culture

- Works council and other employee representatives

Kletti and Schumacher consider the holistic nature to be an essential factor. "Holistic thinking is guaranteed if the processes are fully known and understood, and if mutual links and interfaces are taken into account in improvement strategies. The improvement of individual process steps along a value chain with regard to interfaces is the basis for a positive and holistic development of the overall process."[22]

Just as it is impossible to be partially pregnant, so it is with the implementation of partial Lean: you can only have it or you have it. That's why the holistic approach is mentioned because Lean runs through all areas of a company. You may be able to approach a single project with Lean Management for a short time, but its true potential will only unfold if the overall organization is involved. That is why it is essential to involve employee representatives at an early stage: This can help in explaining the need for change and reducing fears and concerns. Long-term orientation and a stringent goal orientation are also cornerstones of Lean Management, which you have to internalize. The effects of Lean can

---

[22] Kletti, J.; Schumacher, J. (2015): *Die perfekte Produktion - Manufacturing Excellence durch Short Interval Technology (SIT)*, 2nd edition, Springer Verlag, Berlin

already be seen from a short-term perspective, but it will be able to show its full potential in the long term.

The **critical success** factors are those that can determine success and failure. "Lean implementation depends on other critical success factors. Disregarding these critical success factors inevitably leads to failure in achieving the set goals. The Lean philosophy defines the ability of employees to identify waste as fundamental and requires active employee participation. A company whose philosophy does not correspond to the Lean philosophy will not implement sustainable lean structures, but will only pursue the Lean approach parallel to other measures as a short to medium-term initiative."[23]

Lean expert Martin Busse describes the following as critical factors:

- Focus on the Lean Philosophy

- Securing and supporting management

- Respectful interaction with employees

---

[23] Busse, M. (2017): *Implementing Lean Management – ein ganzheitliches Vorgehensmodell zur nachhaltigen Implementierung des Lean Managements in KMU*, p. 135

- Seeing mistakes as an opportunity

- External and internal customer orientation

- Basic understanding of Lean Methods

- Standards as a recurring starting point

- Improvement at the place of action

Although the general factors are quite simple to formulate, the critical factors are those that make up the core of Lean Management. Even if the Lean philosophy is formulated as a new vision of the company, it won't help you if you don't introduce a new way of dealing with mistakes and improvements at the same time. Organizations that manage their employees with instructions will have greater problems than those that give employees a great deal of responsibility.

9.1 Factors That Can Make Lean Implementation Difficult

Even if you consider the critical and general success factors and have started your Lean Management project, it can always happen that there are bigger and smaller stumbling blocks on your way.

Lean can motivate employees incredibly because they get responsibility and see effects quite quickly. But as with anything new, it can happen that your enthusiasm and motivation will diminish at some point. If you implement Lean correctly, especially when it comes to the error and improvement culture, you should **experience little fatigue**. However, you should keep your eyes open here as well: There are opportunities for improvement not only in processes but also in management.

> **EXAMPLE:**
>
> A car dealer introduced Lean in all the workshops of his branches. The result was easily visible: the cars were repaired faster, there was less material consumption—partly due to a new method of refilling the engine oil—and each repair was well documented thanks to a new IT solution. Everything went smoothly, but performance began to decline slowly. Repair times were again somewhat longer, although the processes were the same. The car dealer went into the workshops and watched the employees: "They did their job, and they did it well," but he noticed a lack of enthusiasm. He asked the mechanics how they felt and what they lacked. Their answer was that the new system was

In a small company there is indeed a danger that at some point the opportunities for improvement will be exhausted and the work in Lean Management will then become a routine. Then the only thing you can do is sit down with the employees and ask them what kind of challenges they are looking for and discuss how this fits in with Lean. In the example of mechanics, they wanted more training, especially in electronics and technology. This brought a pleasant change and motivated them more.

Another problem that may arise is the **lack of middle management support**. Even if everyone at the preparatory meetings says they are on board and that they understand the Lean philosophy, some people may not want to put this theory into practice. There are many reasons for this, one of the most common being that they see their position threatened. If you already have this danger in mind, you can try to involve middle management more closely during the planning phase and address concerns.

The same applies to the other levels, by the way: Too often the introduction of Lean (and other new methods) is only a **lip service to leadership** and is not implemented at the top. Particularly in SMEs, owners sometimes think that organizational changes do not affect the company itself. That is naturally wrong: The fish stinks from the head, says an old proverb. If you yourself are not in a position to live the philosophy, then how can your employees do it?

A lack of support from above is therefore also a factor when the **lowest levels in a company**—the so-called shop floor—**slow down a project**. Other reasons could be that Lean is still understood as a method for personnel reduction. Employees think that an improvement might rationalize their job and are therefore more cautious. It can also happen that the new working methods are not sufficiently and clearly communicated by the management. You will have to do a lot of work here and involve the employees on site from the very beginning. Top-down control almost always leads to resistance: Employees do not feel responsible or refuse to participate in the process because they usually only have to carry out instructions.

The speed at which Lean is introduced can also be a braking factor. If changes occur too quickly, employees may feel overwhelmed. If, on the other hand, the introduction takes too long, the enthusiasm decreases faster because no effects are visible, and therefore the advantages cannot be appreciated. It will be difficult for you to estimate the right speed at the beginning. You will have no choice but to always have an ear for your employees and to constantly evaluate whether you are on the right track, especially in the initial phase.

Piotr Jedynak identified some special features of the introduction of Lean in small and medium-sized companies and described them as supporting and hindering factors.[24]

Advantages	Disadvantages
Faster communication	Insufficient financial resources
Uniform organizational structure	Not enough qualified employees

---

[24] Jedynak, P. (2015): *Lean Management implementation – Determinant factors and experience. In: Journal of Management,* vol. 1, no. 1, pp. 51-64

Great flexibility	Dependence on personal ties
Easy response to customer requests	Little knowledge of entrepreneurship
Great influence on employees	Fluctuations in raw materials and supplier prices
Being able to make quick decisions	Poor cash flow and time management
Innovative atmosphere	Decisions are made intuitively, not based on data
Support with changes	Holding on to old processes and structures

Other authors[25] see the following points as obstacles to implementation:

- Traditional thinking and working structures

---

[25] von Eckardstein, D.; Kasper, H.; Mayrhofer, W. (1999): *Management*, Schäffer-Poeschel

- Inadequate knowledge and limited understanding of Lean Management

- Lack of support from top management

- Stereotyped design concept

- Implementation speed too high

- Strong opposition in middle management

- Lack of ability to work in a team

- Management role problems

- Limited understanding of process thinking, customer proximity and a wrong understanding of quality

Here the circle closes: The best methods and concepts will not take you any further, unless there is also a change in the awareness of employees and management.

9.2 Measuring Success in Lean

After you have introduced Lean, you will probably notice quite a bit of change, either because you have probably restructured or because production has already become more efficient. But percentage improvements are only one way to measure the success of Lean. Heinz-Jürgen Klepzig is an expert in Lean Management who compiled some success measurements that have proven themselves.

The main features he saw are:

- C2C measurement (Cash-to-Cash Cycle)

- Cash flow measurement

- Yield measurement

When Toyota introduced its production system, the focus was on improving C2C times. This shows the time that elapses between the purchase of the stored goods and the revenue from sales. Actually, there is a formula to calculate it:

Cash to Cash Cycle Time =
Days Sales Outstanding + Inventory Days of Supply
- Days Payable Outstanding

These are important key figures for you to see how successful Lean is in production as well as in wholesale and retail. By the way, this is also possible in the service sector. Here you replace the Inventory Days with unfinished work and outstanding customer acquisitions. This is not exactly the same, but you can at least derive a trend of whether your numbers improve or not.

Cash flow is one of the biggest problems small and medium-sized companies face today. Suppliers are pushing for fast payment and customers prefer to pay invoices on a monthly basis. Many bridging loans are requested because the cash flow is too small. You should therefore keep an eye on the cash flow, which should actually improve after the introduction of Lean. But Klepzig also warns against concentrating solely on this: "However, the cause-and-effect effect of Lean measures on cash flow changes can only be recorded to a limited extent, since improvements in results can also be achieved without Lean, for example through sales-related sales increases or purchasing-related cost reductions."

The same considerations apply to yield measurement. Here, too, you can see changed numbers, but it won't be easy to assign them to specific Lean Measures: "The monetary cost tracking of the processes in a company generally takes place via different forms of cost accounting." However, the use of the traditional cost approach commonly used in most companies leads to major problems when recording Lean Results. The main reason for this is that the guidelines and metrics for the usual forms of cost accounting (cost centre approach: increasing efficiency through economies of scale) do not correspond to the characteristics and requirements of a Lean Business unit or company (process approach: improving the process flow through economies of flow).[26]

---

[26] Klepzig, H.-J. (2018): *Lean Management in der Praxis – Kritische Darstellung der Kernelemente und Erfolgsmessung*, p. 42

Value Flows

In order for costs to be accurately recorded, the values must also be noted where they occur. In Lean Management and Lean Production, the so-called **value flows** are measured. Lean accounting, or value flow calculation, takes value flows into account. These can include, for example, several products with similar production steps. The value flow then consists of the costs incurred in each step.

EXAMPLE:

A furniture manufacturer has in its catalogue upholstered furniture, tables, beds and cupboards. Upholstered furniture includes sofas and armchairs. These two form a product family. As part of Lean Production, improvements have been introduced, including Just-in-Time production instead of, for example, determining the costs for all raw materials; only those costs incurred for the production of armchairs and sofas are recorded, and this is done in a holistic manner. This can look like the following:

- Raw materials (wood, textiles, fillings)

- Delivery costs

- Cutting textiles and cutting wood

- Sewing

- Frame production

- Upholstery

- Pre-assembly

- Assembly

- Dispatch from factory

- Delivery for sales

Every area entails labor costs and the necessary machinery and materials. This calculation does not include any pro-rata costs from company operations, because you want to know whether the value flow is successful. The advantage of this type of cost accounting is that it operates parallel to the process and is therefore also on the Lean Line. As a result, you can now compare these costs with sales and see how profitable the process is.

However, there are other key figures that can illustrate the success quite well. In "Practical Lean Accounting" there is a table that summarizes the different indicators.

For a production, it may look something like this:

Key figures	Last week	This week	Target
Units per employee	36.17	51.2	50.0
Timely delivery	97%	98%	98%
Factory to warehouse days	13	19	15
Average product costs	423 Euro	398 Euro	400 Euro
Receivables per day	35	33	34

With tables like this, you can see the progress of the most important Lean Elements, but of course you can still adapt them to your needs. In most cases, not only the operational costs and expenses are recorded but also the financial and the capacities.

In software development, for example, there is no stock, only program parts that have not yet been accepted by the customer or software that has been developed but not yet sold. This is how expenses per patient are measured in the hospital sector.

Another example is cost deployment. Here, a cost analysis is introduced that identifies process-oriented waste in the performance processes of a company, filters out priorities for improvement approaches, and identifies measures for improvement.

In step 1, the **total costs** per considered process are recorded.

In step 2, a **loss matrix** is created that records the main types of losses per process, which are determined by measurement or estimation based on size.

In step 3, the causes ("Why?") for the losses determined in step 2 are determined according to the **cause-and-effect principle**. Causing losses, e.g. insufficient material quality, can result in poor plant and work productivity as well as extra costs for the loss matrix.[27]

In some Lean Seminars it is taught that measurements contribute to waste because they do not support the actual process. This may be true when you look at the

---

[27] Klepzig, H.-J. (2018): *Lean Management in der Praxis – Kritische Darstellung der Kernelemente und Erfolgsmessung*, p. 47

process itself but not when you try to get an overall picture. Even if cost accounting in many companies sometimes takes on bizarre proportions, in the end you need figures that can prove improvements or declines.

Heinz-Jürgen Klepzig summarized how successful each of the measurement types are and how easy they are to implement in a table.

	Comprehensibility Cause and Effect	Cost of Preparation	Implentation Expense	Significance
C2C	high	low	low	high
Cashflow	medium	medium	medium	medium
Cost Deployment	low	high	high	high
Lean Accounting	medium	medium	medium	high
Cycle Time	high	low	low	medium

low ● medium ● high ●

Comparison of Lean Performance Measurement Types [28]

It quickly becomes clear that the lead time, which is so popular with most Lean Gurus, is one of the best key figures, also because it is easy to execute. C2C, on the other hand, is more meaningful, and the same applies

---

[28] Eigene Darstellung in Anlehnung an Klepzig, H.-J. (2018): *Lean Management in der Praxis – Kritische Darstellung der Kernelemente und Erfolgsmessung*, p. 50

to Lean Accounting. The effort to implement cost deployment is quite large, so you will usually find it in companies whose main problems are cost pressure or in large companies that have human resources.

10. Summary

If you are so interested in Lean Management that you want to implement it in your own company, then we hope this book will give you some help. The philosophy behind Lean can be found in many companies, especially in industries with high cost pressure; there is no other choice than to improve efficiency and reduce costs with such methods.

However, changing old ways of thinking is a slow process, and especially in big companies you will often encounter resistance when it comes to radical changes. At times, it helps to highlight the success stories and show that Lean works and also works in environments that are otherwise dominated by traditional ways of working.

One such example is **Honda** in Southeast Asia: In most countries such as Thailand, Indonesia and Malaysia repair shops are small garages at the roadside, usually equipped to change tires or oil and living from hand to mouth. The owner usually owns the business and repairs the car himself, but there is no real training as a bicycle mechanic or car mechanic. Honda (and also Yamaha) quickly realized that the workshop concept, as it is known in Japan, was not dependent on what had been done. They therefore organized workshops at dealerships with structured and organized workplaces, introduced a control book and checklists, and trained employees in Lean Processes. It turned out that even inexperienced mechanics were grateful to be able to work in a professional environment with clear processes.

The example above is meant to show that too often the obstacle is the doubt and not the environment and the employees. When employees see the benefits that Lean can bring and don't have to fear that their jobs are threatened, they will often be quicker to get involved than the management itself.

Friedrich Graf-Götz and Hand Glatz already dealt with the basics of Lean in 2001 in their book on the design of organizations, and formulated basic conditions that an organization must bring with it if it is to successfully implement Lean:[29]

- Orientation of all activities towards the customer (customer orientation)

- Focus on your strengths

- Optimization of business processes

- Continuous Improvement of Quality (Continuous Improvement Process, CIP)

- Internal Customer Orientation as a Corporate Mission

- Personal responsibility, empowerment and teamwork

- Decentralized, customer-oriented structures

- Leadership is a service to the employee

- Open information and feedback processes

- Change of attitude and culture in the company (Kaikaku)

---

[29] Graf-Götz, F.; Glatz, H. (2003): *Organisation gestalten – Neue Wege und Konzepte für Organisationsentwicklung und Selbstmanagement*, 4th edition, Beltz Verlag

You can use this list as a kind of daily reminder because it summarizes the essential points very well.

It is not for nothing that customer orientation comes first. It causes the greatest difficulties for most companies because the point of view changes completely. So, if you have been convinced that you offer great products or services, then you may learn through customer orientation that this is not the case.

A great example of how you can be too confident about yourself was shown by **Coca-Cola** in 1985: They wanted to meet Pepsi's growing market share and launched a new, sweeter tasting New Coke. The reaction was devastating: Nobody wanted this new cola; the customers blew up. After only three months, the original cola formula was used again. However, some in the company did not want to receive advice and continued with the new cola as Cola II until 1992.

No matter whether you want to introduce new products or services or change existing ones, if your company has switched to Lean Management, you won't make such mistakes because you have already understood the customer's perspective and needs.

Lean Management is currently a much-loved and popular method, but it is only one of many. Not every company has the right basic conditions described above, and sometimes you have to create them in order to introduce Lean Production. The main work lies with the management: if the Lean Philosophy is anchored at the level of management, then it will be easier to meet the other conditions as well.

Maximilian Tündermann

Bibliography

Bagattini, M. F. (2017): *Lean Management – auch in der Arztpraxis von Vorteil!* URL: https://saez.ch/de/article/doi/saez.2017.05199 [Date of Reference: 16-12-2018]

Blank, S. (2013): Why the Lean Start-Up Changes Everything. URL: https://hbr.org/2013/05/why-the-lean-start-up-changes-everything [Date of Reference: 13-11-2018]

Busse, M. (2017): *Implementing Lean Management – ein ganzheitliches Vorgehensmodell zur nachhaltigen Implementierung des Lean Managements in KMU*

detektierbar.de (2016): 5S Sortiment – Lean Management. URL: https://detektierbar.de/5s-sortiment.html [Date of Reference: 27-12-2018]

Dekier, L. (2012): *The Origins and Evolution of Lean Management System*

Deranek, K.; Chopra, S.; Mosher, G. A. (2017): *Lean Adoption in Small and Medium Enterprise Validation*

Gartner, W. J. (2002): *Management - Einführung in Management, Kommunikation und Personalwirtschaft*, Oldenbourg Wissenschaftsverlag GmbH

Graf-Götz, F.; Glatz, H. (2003): *Organisation gestalten – Neue Wege und Konzepte für Organisationsentwicklung und Selbstmanagement*, 4th edition, Beltz Verlag

Jedynak, P. (2015): *Lean Management implementation – Determinant factors and experience*. In: *Journal of Management*, vol. 1, no. 1, pp. 51-64

Kaizenworld (2016): Kaikaku. URL:
https://www.kaizenworld.com/kaizen-blog/kaikaku.html
[Date of Reference: 21-11-2018]

Keith, D.: Schlanke Unternehmen – Was Lean Management
für die Mitarbeiter bedeutet. URL: https://www.business-
wissen.de/artikel/schlanke-unternehmen-was-lean-
management-fuer-die-mitarbeiter-bedeutet/ [Date of
Reference: 10-12-2018]

Kletti, J.; Schumacher, J. (2015): *Die perfekte Produktion -
Manufacturing Excellence durch Short Interval Technology
(SIT)*, 2nd edition, Springer Verlag, Berlin

Klepzig, H.-J. (2018): *Lean Management in der Praxis –
Kritische Darstellung der Kernelemente und Erfolgsmessung*

Kolf, F. (2016): Rügenwalder Mühler, Meica, Herta – Es geht
um die fleischlose Wurst. URL:
https://www.handelsblatt.com/unternehmen/handel-
konsumgueter/ruegenwalder-muehle-meica-herta-es-geht-
um-die-fleischlose-wurst/14448496.html [Date of
Reference: 07-12-2018]

McKinsey (2011): *Lean Management – New frontiers for
financial institutions*

Mc Kinsey (2014): *The Lean Management Enterprise – A
system for daily progress, meaningful purpose, and lasting
value*

Mrunal (2014): Lean Production at McDonalds. URL:
http://cmuscm.blogspot.com/2014/09/lean-production-at-
mcdonalds.html [Date of Reference: 28-10-2018]

Ohno, T. (1988): *Toyota Production System – Beyond Large-Scale Production*, Productivity Press, Cambridge/Massachusetts

Rishi et al. (2018): *Implementing the Lean Framework in a Small & Medium & Enterprise (SME) – A case Study in Printing Press*, IOP Publishing, IOC Conf. Ser., volume 376, conference 1

riss Consulting (2016): Qualitätsmanagement. URL: http://www.riss.de/consulting/qualitaetsmanagement/ [Date of Reference: 24-11-2018]

Robinson, N. (2015): How Zara used Lean to become the largest fashion retailer. URL: https://www.linkedin.com/pulse/how-zara-used-lean-become-largest-fashion-retailer-nathan-robinson/ [Date of Reference: 05-12-2018]

Soni, P. (2015): Managing Walmart's Supply Chain – Cross-Docking and Other Tools. URL: https://marketrealist.com/2015/02/managing-walmarts-supply-chain-cross-docking-tools [Date of Reference: 17-11-2018]

Staufen AG (2014): Ein guter Weg um Lean Production in kleinen und mittelgroßen chinesischen Unternmehmen (SMEs) zu starten: Das Komzept der flexiblen Montagezelle. URL: https://www.staufen.ag/de/unternehmen/news-events/news/newsdetail/2014/08/ein-guter-weg-um-lean-production-in-kleinen-und-mittelgrossen-chinesischen-unternehmen-smes-zu-star/ [Date of Reference: 12-12-2018]

Tsõgankova, T. (2014): *Lean Implementation in Estonian SMEs based on the example of the company Narva Tes Plus*

von Eckardstein, D.; Kasper, H.; Mayrhofer, W. (1999): *Management*, Schäffer-Poeschel

Wilson, L. (2013): Six Qualities of Lean Leadership. URL: https://www.industryweek.com/continuous-improvement/six-qualities-lean-leadership [Date of Reference: 01-12-2018]

Wujec, T. (2010): Build a tower, build a team. URL: https://www.ted.com/talks/tom_wujec_build_a_tower [Date of Reference: 25-10-2018]

www.ingramcontent.com/pod-product-compliance
Lightning Source LLC
La Vergne TN
LVHW011303210726
843509LV00016B/706